Legends of the Sea

Sea Mysteries

Siân Smith

Chicago, Illinois

www.heinemannraintree.com
Visit our website to find out
more information about
Heinemann-Raintree books.

To order:

☎ Phone 888-454-2279

💻 Visit www.heinemannraintree.com
to browse our catalog and order online.

Edited by Rebecca Rissman, Nancy Dickmann,
and Siân Smith
Designed by Joanna Hinton Malivoire and Ryan Frieson
Original illustrations ©Capstone Global Library 2010
Illustrated by Mendola Ltd
Picture research by Tracy Cummins
Production control by Victoria Fitzgerald
Originated by Capstone Global Library Ltd
Printed and bound in China by Leo Paper Products Ltd

14 13 12 11 10
10 9 8 7 6 5 4 3 2 1

Library of Congress Cataloging-in-Publication Data
Smith, Siân.
Sea mysteries / Siân Smith. p. cm. -- (Legends of the sea)
Includes bibliographical references and index.
 ISBN 978-1-4109-3786-5 (hc)
ISBN 978-1-4109-3791-9 (pb)
1. Adventure and adventurers. 2. Curiosities and wonders.
3. Seafaring life. I. Title.
 G525.S574 2011
 001.94--dc22

Acknowledgments
The author and publishers are grateful to the following for
permission to reproduce copyright material: akg-images
p.18 (© Peter Connolly); Alamy p.21 (© Michael Robertson);
Corbis p.9; Getty Images pp.5 (David Fleetham), 13
(Keystone), 19 (Popperfoto), 22 (Mark Kolbe), 25 (Brandon
Cole), 26 (© Philipp Maitz); Library of Congress Prints
and Photographs Division p.7; National Geographic Stock
p.27 (Norbert Wu/Minden Pictures); Shutterstock pp.10 (©
Mana Photo), 14 (© JirkaBursik), 26 (© Yakobchuk Vasyl,
29 (© musicman); The Art Archive p.23 (John Meek); The
Bridgeman Art Library International pp.12, 16 (© Look and
Learn).

Every effort has been made to contact copyright holders of
any material reproduced in this book. Any omissions will
be rectified in subsequent printings if notice is given to the
publisher.

All the Internet addresses (URLs) given in this book were
valid at the time of going to press. However, due to the
dynamic nature of the Internet, some addresses may have
changed, or sites may have changed or ceased to exist since
publication. While the author and Publishers regret any
inconvenience this may cause readers, no responsibility for
any such changes can be accepted by either the author or the
Publishers.

Some words are shown in bold, **like this**. You can find
out what they mean by looking in the glossary.

Contents

Mysteries at Sea

Strange things can happen at sea. A **mystery** is something that we haven't been able to explain. Can you solve any of the sea mysteries here?

Do **ghosts** sail the seas?

What happened on the *Mary Celeste*?

Why do boats disappear in the **Bermuda Triangle**?

Do mermaids exist?

Is the city of **Atlantis** under the sea?

Read this book to find out some answers!

The Mystery of the Bermuda Triangle

The **Bermuda Triangle** is an area in the Atlantic Ocean. Strange things have happened in the Bermuda Triangle for hundreds of years. Some boats and planes have completely disappeared there...

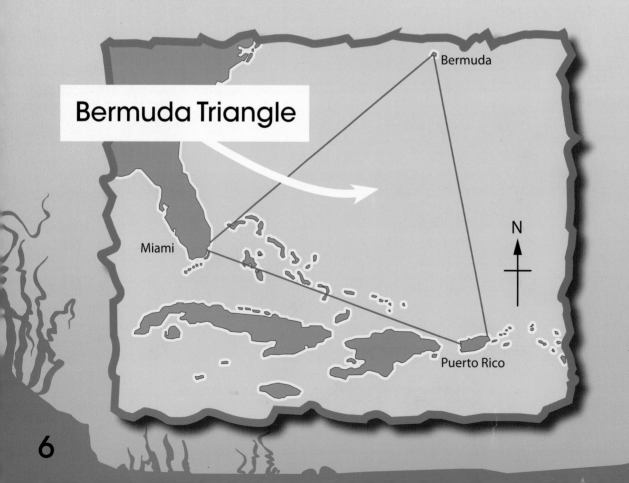

Bermuda Triangle

Bermuda

Miami

N

Puerto Rico

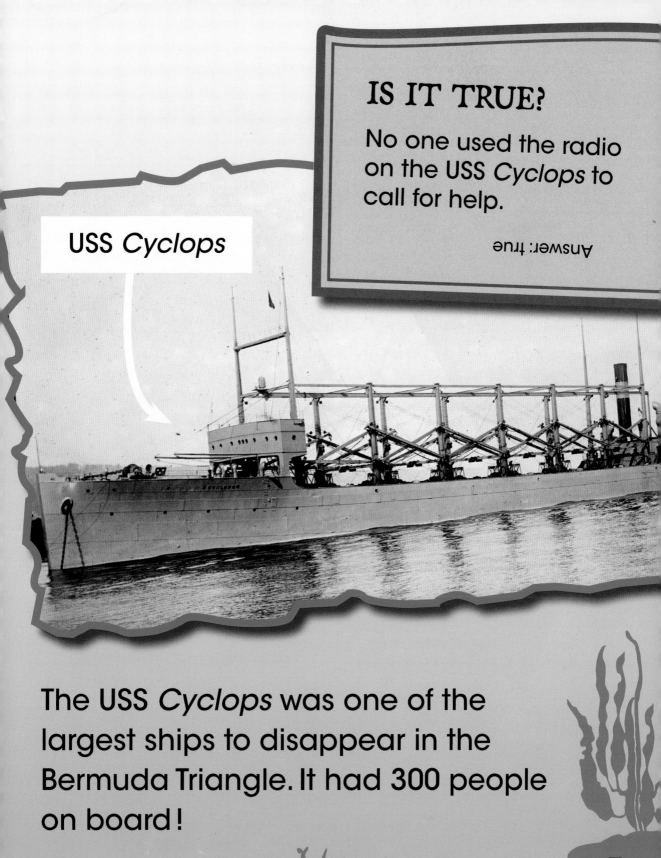

USS *Cyclops*

The USS *Cyclops* was one of the largest ships to disappear in the Bermuda Triangle. It had 300 people on board!

Some people who have been through the **Bermuda Triangle**, say spooky things happened there. Some saw strange lights, huge foaming waves, or mysterious fog.

Compasses show direction, but they can go wrong in the Bermuda Triangle !

Five planes like these all vanished in the Bermuda Triangle.

Why do things disappear in the Bermuda Triangle? Why has no **wreckage**, or parts of the boats and planes, been found?

Solving the Bermuda Triangle Mystery

People have many ideas about what happens in the **Bermuda Triangle**. Which **theory**, or idea, do you think explains the **mystery**?

Bad weather can sometimes cause giant waves.

Theory	Is it true?
Giant waves	Could giant waves swallow up boats?
Aliens	Are ships and planes taken away by aliens?
Gas bubbles	Could giant gas bubbles rising up through the sea make ships sink?

A ship caught in a bubble of gas could disappear without a trace.

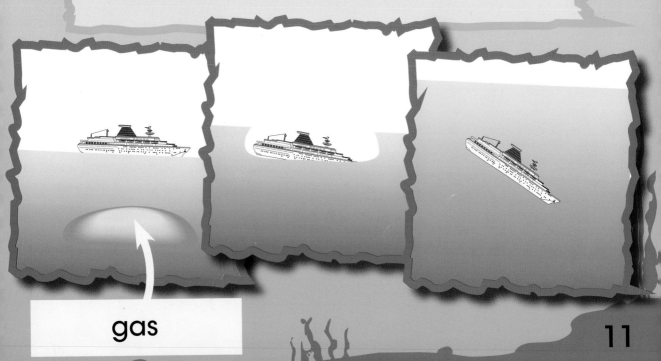

gas

Ghost Ships

A whole ship disappearing at sea sounds strange. The thought of just the people on board vanishing seems even stranger! A **ghost ship** is a ship found with no people on board.

ghost ship

These sailors have just spotted a ghost ship!

Mary Celeste

DID YOU KNOW?

The *Mary Celeste* is a famous ghost ship. The ship was fine when it was found, but all the people on board were missing!

What Happened on the Mary Celeste?

It seems that the people on the *Mary Celeste* probably left in a lifeboat, which then sank. The big **mystery** is: why did they leave the ship? What were they scared of?

exploding barrels

pirates

Was it...	What do people think?
Pirates?	Probably not. Valuables were left on the ship.
Exploding barrels?	Maybe. There were barrels on board that could have exploded.
An earthquake making big waves?	Maybe. Things found on the ship were very wet.

giant waves

Ghosts at Sea

Some people say they have seen ghostly ships with **ghosts** on board. Do these sorts of **ghost ships** exist?

DID YOU KNOW?
Sailors on the *Flying Dutchman* are said to be cursed to sail forever.

There are **legends** of a ship called the *Flying Dutchman*. They say the ghost of the ship has been seen, even though the ship was destroyed in a terrible storm.

Sunken Cities

There is a famous **mystery** about a lost city called **Atlantis**. People say the city sank into the sea after a terrible earthquake.

This is what one artist thought Atlantis might have looked like.

Plato

DID YOU KNOW?

We only know about Atlantis from a man called Plato. No one knows if Plato was writing about a real place.

IS IT TRUE?

Weapons from Atlantis have been found.

Answer: false

19

People have searched for **Atlantis** for hundreds of years. A place on the island of Crete sounded a lot like Atlantis, but it didn't disappear into the sea. The search for Atlantis goes on today...

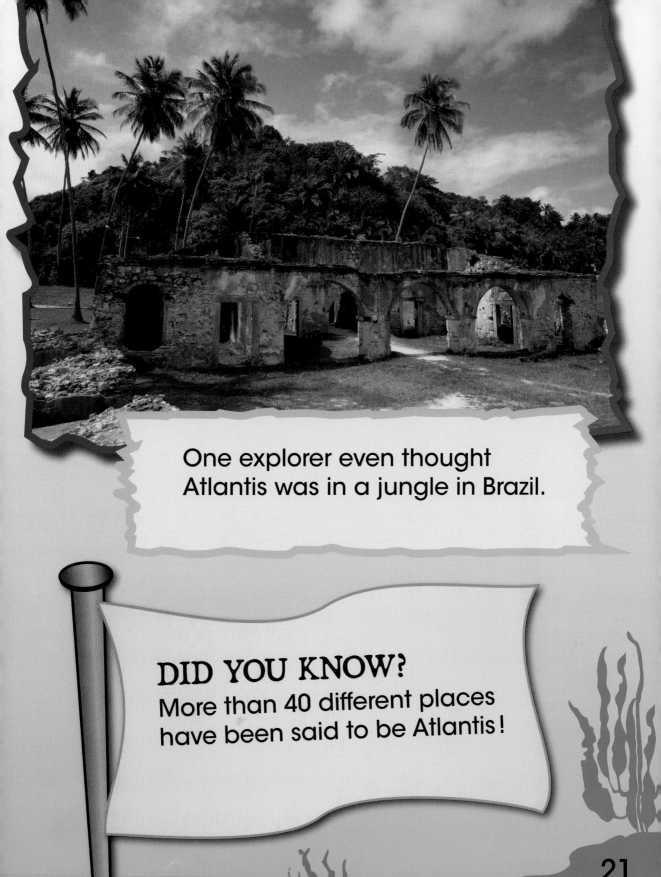

One explorer even thought
Atlantis was in a jungle in Brazil.

DID YOU KNOW?
More than 40 different places
have been said to be Atlantis!

Mysterious Mermaids

Legends about mermaids say they have the upper body of a woman and the tail of a fish. Some say mermaids are kind creatures who have saved sailors. Others say they cause trouble. Do mermaids exist?

DID YOU KNOW?

About 120 years ago, hundreds of people on a Scottish island said they saw a mermaid. They called it the Deerness Mermaid.

Manatees are animals that have a lot in common with mermaids. Could mermaid-spotters have seen manatees instead?

manatee

DID YOU KNOW?
Columbus wrote that mermaids are not as beautiful as people think. He could have been talking about manatees!

Mysteries of the Deep

The sea is a huge place and we have only explored a small part of it. What could be lurking deep at the bottom of the sea is another **mystery** waiting to be solved.

Deep sea cameras have taken pictures of strange new creatures, such as this Angler fish.

IS IT TRUE?

There are some parts of the sea that we cannot explore yet. People can die if they go down too deep.

Answer: true

Detective Tips

We've been trying to solve sea **mysteries** for hundreds of years. Your ideas are as important as anyone else's.

Why not become a sea mystery detective yourself?

Collect

Get all the information you can. Search books, museums, and the Internet.

Think in new ways

Ask what else you would need to know to solve the mystery.

Question

Remember to ask if what you are reading is true. Where did the information come from?

Glossary

Atlantis a lost city that some people believe disappeared under the sea

Bermuda Triangle an area of water and islands in the Atlantic Ocean. Some boats and airplanes have disappeared in the Bermuda Triangle without leaving a trace behind.

compass piece of equipment that shows direction. Compasses point to the north.

ghost spirit of someone or something that has passed away

ghost ship either a real ship that is sailing with no people on board or the ghost of a ship

legend story that started long ago. Legends can be true or made up.

mystery something we haven't been able to explain

theory idea

wreckage the bits and pieces left behind when something has been damaged

Find Out More

Find out

Where might you see glowing water?

Books

Holly Wallace, *Can Science Solve...? The Mystery of Atlantis*, Heinemann Library, 2nd Edition, 2007.

Kathryn Walker, *Unsolved! Mysteries of the Bermuda Triangle*, Crabtree Publishing Company, 2008.

Jane Yolen and Heidi Elisabeth Yolen Stemple, *The Mary Celeste: An Unsolved Mystery from History*, Simon & Schuster Children's Publishing, 2002.

Websites

www.crystalinks.com/bermuda_triangle.html

Find out about the strange things that have happened in the Bermuda Triangle and how people have tried to explain them.

www.maryceleste.net/

Investigate the mystery of the *Mary Celeste* and explore information from the time.

www.robertosozzani.it/Dugong/leggendeEN.html

Learn about dugongs—creatures that some people thought were mermaids. Hear what a dugong sounds like on this website.

Index